W9-AEW-612

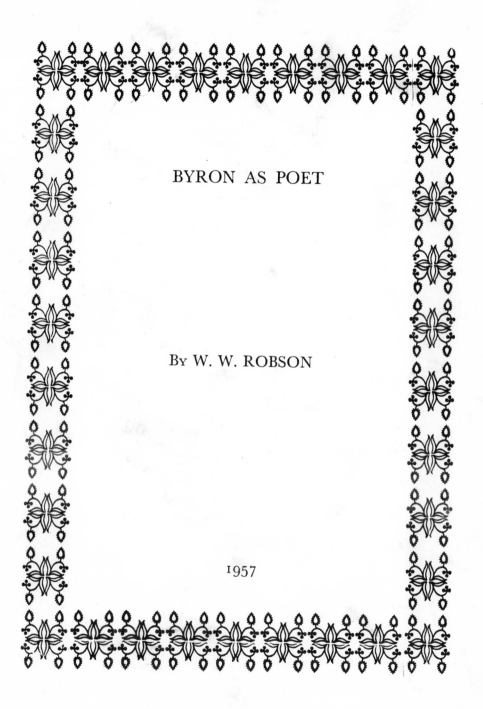

BYRON AS POET

By W. W. ROBSON

1957

BYRON AS POET

By W. W. ROBSON

Read 16 January 1957

TO entitle a lecture 'Byron as Poet' presupposes that Byron is a subject for literary criticism. But this is not self-evident. Byron's biographers, whether they go to work in the spirit of Mr. Quennell and Sir Harold Nicolson, or in that of Mr. Wilson Knight, use his poetry quite freely as direct evidence for a biographical thesis. And they are justified in doing so: that, indeed, is the first critical observation to be made about Byron's poetry. Whatever reservations may accompany the judgement that Byron is not essentially a *dramatic* artist, it will surely be agreed that his genius was not such as to issue, characteristically, in self-sufficient works of art containing in themselves (in Coleridge's phrase) the reasons why they are so and not otherwise. No clear line of demarcation can be drawn between discussion of 'the man', and discussion of 'the work': Byron's personality is as much the subject for a critical essay on Byron, as it is for a biography. Our sense of the individuality of the artist is inseparable from our sense of the human case that underlies the art. But this is not to grant that the critic need concern himself much with the latest details of pathological excavation; or even with 'author-psychology' as that is ordinarily understood; since he is concerned, not so much with the reasons for the peculiarities of Byron's poetry, as with their nature. To describe this permits of no freer and looser approach than should be adopted with any poet. And to produce at the same time the analysis and judgement which a correct description entails, is at once the purpose of, and the justification for, reference to Byron's personality in a critical essay; in an essay, that is, which attempts to communicate with the reader whose interest is in poetry and not, primarily, in *Kulturgeschichte*, psycho-pathology, or scandal.

Not that an interest in Byron's poetry needs justifying at present; it suffers neither from neglect, nor excessive depreciation; Byron is not only read about, he is read: as much, I imagine, as any other English poet. (I mean, read by others besides professional students of poetry.) But there seems to be missing, in current appraisals of Byron, a determination to define his peculiar qualities as a poet, and, still more, a recognition that the defining is difficult. Biographical studies of various aspects of Byron, and phases of his life, have been amply provided; and they are certainly needed, perhaps more in Byron's case than in that of any other English poet; but the extant ones fail, it seems to me, in a respect which is important even to the student of his life, as distinct from his poetry; they do not convey something essential to the understanding of this man, in that they do not record any first-hand perception of why he is worth discussing, or how he should be discussed, other than as a psychological problem or a fascinating 'period' subject. And perhaps this lack of concentrated critical interest in Byron's poetry, that is, in the precise character of what it has to offer to us here and now in the twentieth century, may be correlated (in Quennell's and Nicolson's books at any rate) with their seeming want of profound sympathy with Byron as a person, or a sense of him as a human force.

No one could accuse Mr. Wilson Knight of this last deficiency. And if the book he plans to bring out on Byron's poetry has the quality of his lecture on *Byron's Dramatic Prose* (University of Nottingham, Byron Foundation Lecture 1953), our inward understanding of the poetic/prophetic character of the Pilgrim of Eternity will be much increased. What worries me in what he has said so far, is that *his* Byron, existing so completely on an apocalyptic dimension to which most of us can have but little access, not only seems to be without some familiar Byronic traits, but apparently communicates with his interpreter quite as satisfactorily in what are surely inferior poems, as in impressive ones. We must wait for Mr. Wilson Knight's coming book, before passing judgement; but one is a little worried, when things so varied in character, substance, and artistic merit are used so confidently to establish a thesis; the argument incurs more suspicion from the judicious admirer of Byron, than it would if it had been presented with more constant regard to the varying quality, significance, and value of the evidence. To bring out this variety is to recognize the need to discriminate and distinguish; and this recognition is as necessary to the critic as the warm sympathy and fullness of response which Mr. Wilson Knight's work shows so abundantly. If he is going to ask us to swallow Byron whole, I hope he will serve him up well seasoned with the salt of criticism.

The ideal spirit in which the critic of Byron should set about his task is well suggested, in my opinion, by these two quotations

from a critic enjoying the peculiar advantages, as a critic writing
in English on English poetry, of a European point of view: I
am thinking of George Santayana, who showed in his criticism
all the Latin virtues, without many of the Latin limitations. I
quote here two passages from his letters, apropos of Byron; the
first written when he was young, the second in later life. In a
letter of 1887 he writes:

> I always have found a great difficulty in feeling the glow of admiration
> and the glow of loyalty towards the same persons. Admiration comes
> from qualities, and loyalty from obligations. What one admires are
> abstractions and sides of character, but one is loyal to the whole man,
> as to one who is knit into one's own life. Perhaps I ought to confess that
> I worship one hero, although as a man out of history he oughtn't to count.
> I mean Byron. Towards Byron, I do feel a combination of admiration
> and loyalty. I admire what he is in himself, and I am full of recognition
> for what he has been to me. For you must know, Byron is my first friend
> among the poets, and my favourite.[1]

That, of course, is the voice of youthful enthusiasm; but coming
from Santayana, it does bring home to us vividly the Latin, the
European significance of Byron—one sees this in Santayana's
own poetry—and the intensity and strength of Byron's European
appeal. Many years later, however, having been 're-reading
the whole of *Don Juan*', Santayana writes to Richard C. Lyon:
'Some parts bored me, the invectives especially; but, as you say,
he is witty, and his rhymes sometimes surpassingly clever. *But
he did not respect himself or his art as much as they deserved.*' (Italics
mine.) It is that last sentence which condenses an essential
criticism of *Don Juan*. And somewhere between this final attitude
of critical reserve, and the earlier blend of 'admiration' and
'loyalty' towards 'one who is knit into one's own life', the critic's
correct position seems to me to be found; he must be capable of
a real response to Byron's appeal, which does not preclude, or
leave finally in abeyance, a sense of dissatisfaction, disappoint-
ment, and disillusion. He must, in fact, be prepared to recapitu-
late, in his experience of Byron's poetry, something of that
general process of maturing, often painfully and with loss as well
as gain, which parts of *Don Juan* itself unforgettably record; a
development necessarily implying the renunciation of much that
delighted our youth.

The doubt that afflicts us, after we have mentally gone over
our impressions of Byron's poetry, crystallizes into the question:
how much of it *is* poetry? And this leads to the further question;

[1] *Letters*, ed. Cory, p. 16.

has Byron as poet enough self-knowledge and command of his experience to be judged a *great* poet? These questions remain to trouble us, even if we confine our attention to the things that, by general agreement, constitute—at any rate for the modern reader—the main body of Byron's achievement in verse: *Don Juan*, the *Vision of Judgment*, and *Beppo* (and, I would add, the later cantos of *Childe Harold*.) Of these, the *Vision of Judgment* comes the nearest to being a thing done and complete, an object for criticism by itself and in itself; and the *Vision of Judgment* is hardly a great creative work. *Don Juan* is naturally what most of us would cite in support of a high estimate of Byron's poetic genius; but one's established impression of it is ominously coloured by that sense of dissatisfaction recorded by Santayana. The casualness, or irresponsibility, of its *procédé* may be the condition for the poem's virtues, but it is not itself always, or even often, a virtue. One feels in reading much of *Don Juan* that it must have come very easily, and this feeling shades into the judgment '*too* easily'; a great work of art must contain themes which have offered a resistance to the artist, as well as being attractive to him. I do not dispute that *Don Juan* is very entertaining, one of the most readable—if not very re-readable—of long poems; I am concerned at the moment only with the very high claims for it which are made by some of its admirers. I do not think the justice of these claims is by any means self-evident.

Santayana is surely right to link his dissatisfaction with the 'art' of the poem, to his dissatisfaction with the recurrent attitude of self-contempt—the basis perhaps of the intermittent disrespect for humanity in general—which is so striking a feature of Byron's case. This mood bears a relation to the equally typical habit of self-assertion, in that famous rhetorical attitudinizing; a relation which is not one of simple antithesis. All that matters to the critic, of course, is what is *made* of these moods and habits, and the relationships between them, by the creative force of the poet; but he would be a very bold critic who would argue that the moral and emotional predispositions which these moods reflect, are everywhere and uniformly in Byron impersonalized, absolved, or transcended. The case is more complex: everywhere in Byron we find assertion, and the contrasting, yet complementary, abjectness. But then we find too in the mature work, the beginnings of a power to diagnose them; to see his pride, and its less harmful (if less dignified) accompaniments of vanity and conceit, for what they are. And these insights appear often in close quarters with the ignorance of oneself and of other

people which egotism always entails. Similarly, there are obtuse-
nesses and blindnesses, the more disturbing because they will
often occur in the midst of a display of notable sensitiveness,
intelligence, and imagination. An example from life here will
not mean a wanton digression, since in Byron's case (it is not so,
of course, with many other artists) either the art, or the man,
will testify in a fairly straightforward way what each other is
like. How akin to the art of the good novelist is the moral
delicacy, evincing and articulating itself in that constant play of
representation and perception—at once witty and profound—
which determines the whole presentment in those letters to Lady
Melbourne of his 'affair', if such we must call it, with Lady
Frances Webster! What insight into milieu, situation, and character, his own (as the star of the drama) included! And yet,
what a limitation of moral outlook, what a lack of awareness of
self and the people concerned, is there as well! Now it is a real
tribute, if a paradoxical one, to Byron as a responsible being and
a born creative writer, and to what he makes thereby of that little
episode in writing of it, that we speak of these disablements as
we might in criticizing a novelist; that we are tempted to speak
in moral terms, rather than in terms of a neurotic condition. It
is just because of the very great degree to which Byron is obviously
in command of his experience here, that we are led to ask for
evidence of a still fuller and finer control. The apparent absence
of this in life is closely related to the undoubted absence of it in
Byron's writings. But to suggest that Byron's judgement is sometimes blurred by egotism, of one kind or another, is not at all to
contradict the assertion that 'he did not respect himself, or his
art, as much as they deserved'. On the contrary, a lack of true
self-respect, so far from being incompatible with self-love, often
accompanies it. Similarly, the luxury of self-abasement may well
be a corollary of the will to assert oneself.

Attitudes such as those characteristic of Byron are not un-
common; although the opportunity to strike them on so large a
stage, and to act out so completely their consequences, is not
granted to many. At any rate, whatever view we take of Byron's
own character, there can be no doubt that much of the cult of
Byron, in his own time and later, was merely the gratification,
in fantasy, of numerous petty egotisms; the magnifying to heroic
proportions of one's own easy angers, tears, and surrenders; the
indulgence of *saeva indignatio*; and that sense of injured merit
which provides so many occasions for the release of a vindicated
self-pity. Which of us cannot see himself as the hero-victim of

that *besoin de la fatalité* which M. du Bos declares to be the domi-
nant force in Byron's life? And who does not also see, in his more
veracious moments, that this vision is but an illusory enlarge-
ment of his own pettiness? But to see that constantly; and yet
to be unable to resist the recurrent temptation thus to indulge
oneself; and to have also the power to give truly classical expression to both sides of that state of mind and soul—this is Byron's
own case, as distinct from that of many of his admirers and
would-be imitators, and it is a very unusual one. The Byronic
predicament may not be simply or wholly what it purports to
be; but to give both its illusion of itself, and its reality, is a remarkable achievement. It is the achievement of a robust, if not
often very fine, creative intelligence. And so either to castigate
Byron's self-indulgences as an artist, or to condone them, is
equally irrelevant; he himself having done both, with incom-
parable power, in his own poetry: since the wish or need to do
both was very likely a necessary condition for his creative effort.

We must therefore be sedulous, in reconsidering Byron's
achievement in poetry, to keep the general human judgement in
suspense; by way of a recognition that it is not a simple one. It
is impossible not to be constantly incited to commit ourselves
to it, because of the frankly and insistently personal quality of
Byron's characteristic poetry, as shown in both its manner and
its matter. But at least we can avoid that *parti pris* which is
derived from a (very understandable) anti-romantic prejudice.
Mr. Eliot has given us an excellent essay on Byron (in *From
Anne to Victoria*, edited by Bonamy Dobrée). Yet it is to my mind
weakened by the constant intrusion of this prejudice. Thus,
having affirmed that Byron's being a Scot is the most significant
single clue for the student of his poetry, Mr. Eliot is inevitably
led to a comparison with Byron's greatest Scots contemporary.
And the reminder of the human qualities, the moral grandeur,
of Walter Scott—on which Byron himself generously insisted to
Stendhal—only serves to strengthen the critic's initial prejudice
against Byron's disorder. But this kind of human judgement,
made at the outset, and always felt in the background, means
the deflection of criticism. The assessment of Byron's poetry—
this truism is particularly worth repeating and emphasizing in
his case—must begin and end with the poetry.

As the popularizer of Romanticism, Byron the poet has
important European affinities, as well as being a pervasive (if
not always obvious) influence in nineteenth-century English
poetry; and therefore he demands more critical attention in this

role than the poetry it gave rise to perhaps merits intrinsically. No doubt it is the cine-camera passages of *Childe Harold* that accounted for part of its sensational and immediate success, with a public starved of travel; but a more important attraction was the offer of metaphysical and spiritual profundities, the dark hints of hidden depths of sin and guilt, associated—as they are also in the verse-tales which followed—with the impressive and sombre, if somewhat histrionic and self-conscious, *persona* of Byronic legend. The evaluation of this, in its relation to Byron's literary personality as a whole, is not simple. It cannot be dismissed as merely the striking of an attitude.

> With all that chilling mystery of mien,
> And seeming gladness to remain unseen,
> He had (if 'twere not nature's boon) an art
> Of fixing memory on another's heart:
> It was not love perchance, nor hate, nor aught
> That words can image to express the thought;
> But they who saw him did not see in vain,
> And once beheld, would ask of him again;
> And those to whom he spake remember'd well,
> And on the words, however light, would dwell;
> None knew nor how, nor why, but he entwined
> Himself perforce around the hearer's mind;
> There he was stamp'd, in liking, or in hate,
> If greeted once: however brief the date
> That friendship, pity, or aversion knew,
> Still there within the inmost thought he grew.
> You could not penetrate his soul, but found,
> Despite your wonder, to your own he wound;
> His presence haunted still; and from the breast
> He forced an all unwilling interest:
> Vain was the struggle in that mental net,
> His spirit seem'd to dare you to forget!
>
> *(Lara, I. xix)*

No doubt there is some attitudinizing here, but there is also something genuine. One cannot, however, agree with certain French critics that such passages represent a profound self-study, the result of prolonged self-analysis. The effect is either of a man speaking with the conviction of one who is the greatest living authority on a subject, because he has invented it; or of one trying himself out in a role, and discovering as he goes along that it suits him. And the success of this role depends on the awareness of a public predisposed to be impressed by it. Such a public is not likely to notice, or care if it did, the contradictoriness of his apologia, pointed out by Mr. Eliot: the Byronic sinner, the Giaour for example, alternately excuses his wickedness by proclaiming that it is not wickedness, since he has transvalued his values, and by pleading that it is not his fault, but the fault of circumstances. Both the contradictoriness, and the popularity, of the Byronic sinner in this attitude, testify to its origin in rebellious Protestantism; in this case, in the consciousness of a rakish patrician with the emotional habit-pattern of a Presbyterian minister. (Even in Byron's Venice period we are reminded that he was brought up in Aberdeen.)

But it is not as the precise summing-up of an attitude, even a contradictory one, that such Byronic figures are finally significant and influential. Their power lay in the indefiniteness of their *Weltanschauung*: they could be the ready receptacle for the vague emotions of a great variety of temperaments. There is today a prejudice against poetry which expresses only vague emotion; but it should be noted that in Byron's verse, while the emotion may be vague, the statement of it is explicit. And here of course is the unsatisfactoriness of this kind of poetry. Byronism is better expressed in music; there is something about words which is alien to it, their obstinate tendency to particularize. The Byronic mood at its most intense consists of desire and sadness in their simplest, their most general character; to specify what the sadness is about, or what object could satisfy the desire, can only dissipate the mood by recalling those very particulars of experience which it was its consolation to transcend.

And there is not only something unsatisfactory about Byron's Romantic poetry, there is something false. The declamatory style of the 'profound' passages in *Childe Harold* III and IV is at odds with the simultaneous attempt at an inward treatment of the themes. This discrepancy, producing a typical effect of externality, we diagnose as the result of derivativeness; the main source being Wordsworth—though we should probably add Coleridge and Shelley to the list of tributaries. Indeed, the whole of *Childe Harold* is an interesting study in what 'influence' really means—influence of the wrong kind, of course, since Byron's relation to Wordsworth's poetry is not the less but the more parasitic for being probably not conscious. The Romantic element in the poem is an instructive example of how the process of popularization—*vulgarization*—inevitably denatures what it touches. And we still have to note this, even when Byron's materials are most his own, when he is taking his bleeding heart to the tourist-places of Europe in a most un-Wordsworthian fashion.

And yet there is something impressive about the strength and conviction with which Byron does what he does, and one cannot copy out a famous set-piece like the Dying Gladiator without feeling admiration.

> I see before me the Gladiator lie:
> He leans upon his hand—his manly brow
> Consents to death, but conquers agony,
> And his droop'd head sinks gradually low—
> And through his side the last drops, ebbing slow
> From the red gash, fall heavy, one by one,
> Like the first of a thunder-shower; and now
> The arena swims around him—he is gone,
> Ere ceased the inhuman shout which hail'd the wretch who won.
>
> He heard it, but he heeded not—his eyes
> Were with his heart, and that was far away. . . .

This of course is rhetorical writing, but it is a very distinguished rhetoric; there is a great Latin and European tradition behind it, and a national poetry which is not adorned by such things is the poorer, the more provincial. No living poet could write this kind of verse with that degree of strength and conviction; poetry which is both good, and popular, in the way this is, I cannot imagine appearing in the twentieth century. Byron speaks here in the accents of a great European tradition of the public style. But he none the less speaks with his own voice: Arnold, indeed, cited the last two lines of the passage I have quoted, as illustrating Byron's specific quality as a poet; and, in justice to that quality, I will quote again what seem to me two still finer lines:

> He leans upon his hand—his manly brow
> Consents to death, but conquers agony.

If we are compelled, in considering the whole undertaking of *Childe Harold*, to lay stress on the limitations of the rhetorical manner, it is only fair to bring out at the same time what that manner, at its most impressive, can do.

The limitations, of course, were inherent in Byron's conception of poetry when he began *Childe Harold*. The poem contains that striking rhetoric on grand 'public' themes; and even when Harold's philosophical rhapsodizings are in full swing, they are not unimpressive; yet a casual fragment of Byron's prose will often contain more of the true poet's quick, alert, immediate report of experience, than any of the personal declarations of *Childe Harold*, and the reflective moments are in keeping.

Woke, and was ill all day, till I had galloped a few miles. Query—was it the cockles, or what I took to correct them, that caused the commotion? I think both. I remarked in my illness the complete inertion, inaction and destruction of my chief mental faculties. I tried to rouse them, and yet could not—and this is the *Soul*!!! I should believe that it was married to the body, if they did not sympathise so much with each other. If the one rose, when the other fell, it would be a sign that they longed for the natural state of divorce. But as it is, they seem to draw together like post-horses.[1]

It would be hard to divine from *Childe Harold* the variety, range, and above all the intellectual mobility (evinced in the quality of the perceptiveness) of the Byron of the letters and journals.

But this brings us back to Byron's conception of form and style in poetry. *Childe Harold* is unquestionably the work of a very intelligent man; but in poetry the quality of intelligence is the quality of perceptiveness; and the quality of the perceptions in *this* poetry is affected by the mode they are expressed in. And here we have the other way in which Byron is a representative voice of his age; he is not only a popularizer of Romanticism; he is also a poet of the Regency. The living poet and critic to whom he most deferred was Gifford; and, though he has greater scope and force even in his earlier work, he is there the same *kind* of poet as Rogers, Campbell, or Moore, whom he backed against Southey and Wordsworth to 'try the question' with posterity. His staple language, though characterized, even in his earlier work, by the tones of his natural voice, acknowledges an eighteenth-century poetic. And it is afflicted everywhere with the effeteness of a verse-idiom in decline. The style of the earlier eighteenth-century poets, though it seems restricted in comparison with Shakespeare's freedom, gets its vitality partly from one's feeling of its perpetual effort to *hold back* concreteness. The spirit in which those poets wrote is shown in Dr. Johnson's rationalizing analysis of *To be, or not to be* . . . . And the extrusion of Shakespearianism in this verse appears, not as a mere absence of concreteness, but as a positive sense of tension in the effort to reject it. In later eighteenth-century poetry this pressure has relaxed; so that the diction is choked with the accumulated dry husks of a style designed to restrain, which now restrains nothing. And here we have the explanation of Byron's prolixity, his habit of never using one word when three will do. Even in his more mature work, he cannot rely on the single word or phrase to carry any potency of charge; his poetic effects must be cumula-

[1] *Diary*, 27 Feb. 1821.

tive, since they cannot be concentrated. He is capable of, and indeed cultivates, the shape, lucidity, and *ordonnance* of Augustan poetry, but he cannot achieve its distinction of style. Compare any passage of *English Bards* with the best of Dryden or Pope.

We should recall that the Regency is pre-eminently a period of 'good bad poetry'—if we may so designate a species of composition which is neither good, nor bad, nor, in any important sense, poetry. It is the period of *Ye Mariners* and *Hohenlinden*, of *The Stately Homes* and *Casabianca*; a genre to which Byron himself contributes, with his *Destruction of Sennacherib* and other things. To write such poems, with their terrible memorability, requires, together with complete conviction, absolute banality of sentiment, and obvious rhythm, a poetic diction on the point of death. And, varied as are the kinds of badness in Byron's poetry: the schoolboy rhetoric which can be found everywhere in his work, from *Hours of Idleness* to *Don Juan*; the leading-article declamation of *Napoleon's Farewell*; the drawing-room romantic of *Tambourgi, Tambourgi*; the Regency album sentiment; the Augustan platform manner; and modes ranging from the histrionic-profound of *Darkness: a Fragment* at one extreme to the squib and lampoon at the other; all these have in common, besides the invariable energy of Byron, a lack of verbal distinction. Byron is the poet and stylist of a linguistic nadir.

And other discrepancies and falsities can be blamed in part on the period of English literature, of which this diction was the habit. The Regency in literature was a moment of interruption; a time when Romantic feeling had not yet found its social, moral, and religious bearings in the consciousness of the community, or united itself with other new trends in the national life. Romanticism in its first phase was only alive in the experience of a few individuals; there was thus an effect of externality and falsetto when, like Byron, they sought to express the new development of feeling in an idiom which did not grant, in poetry, such primacy to the experience of the individual. And the liberation achieved in the first place by Robert Burns, and in the second by Wordsworth and Coleridge, did not affect the texture of Byron's verse until he had reached a stage when Romantic feeling was not primarily what he had to express.

Byron's earlier poetry, then, apart from its purely biographical significance, has on the whole only a representative importance. All the same, his work even in its later and greater developments, never loses touch with the eighteenth century. Bertrand Russell was wrong in thinking that Byron's cult of Pope, as the supreme poet, was an affectation. (See the chapter on Byron in *A History of Western Philosophy*.) Nothing is clearer or sincerer in Byron's poetry than his admiration for the eighteenth-century order and rationality, for its limpidity and pattern. The pre-eminence of *Don Juan* among his poems is in one respect unfortunate: in that it causes critics to forget that usual concern of Byron's for method, arrangement, and structure, a concern from which *Don Juan*, like its predecessor *Beppo*, is a deliberate exception. It is in diction and rhythm that Byron's earlier poetry shows a difference, and a deterioration, from the best eighteenth-century work. In his verse-tales, which are very entertaining, this may be partially compensated by the energy and easy movement; as in the opening of *The Corsair*:

> O'er the glad waters of the dark blue sea,
> Our thoughts as boundless, and our souls as free,
> Far as the breeze can bear, the billows foam,
> Survey our empire, and behold our home!
> These are our realms, no limits to their sway—
> Our flag the sceptre all who meet obey.
> Ours the wild life in tumult still to range,
> From toil to rest, and joy in every change.

The *élan* of the movement is characteristically Byron's; but the language is merely politician's English. Where anything in the nature of a concentrated effect is wanted, this is painfully obvious; Byron's very forcefulness only accentuates the poverty of the style. We become aware, not so much of the lack of ear which Swinburne complains of in Byron, as the lack of *mouth* (so to speak); delivery of Byron's verse neither liquefies the palate, nor tightens the jawbone; he has no sense of words as physiological facts, more or less subtly co-operating when we pronounce them to create the illusion of meaning-analogues modifying the vocal organs. Where he is successful in more concentrated pieces, as in the bitter *Ode to Napoleon* (1814), verse-form serves merely the purpose of adding emphasis, regularity, and outline to the virtues of discourse. The distinction of Byron's more interesting poems is not that he attained, or even moved towards, a greater plasticity of language; but that, in admitting a fresh range of feelings into his poetry, he introduced new shades and inflexions of the speaking voice; and so, while his staple language is not altered—being still a mixture of conventional poeticism, formal prose qualities, and his own colloquial accent—its effect is different, since it moves with more interesting and more personal rhythms.

By looking at the relation between diction and movement, then, we may study the evolution of Byron's most truly personal and original poetry, the core of his work. A very early poem like *When we two parted* (1808) already shows the close association, in Byron, between the depth or quality of a poem's sentiment and the individuality of its verse-rhythm. The perpetual slight unexpectedness of the measure, the continuous small uncertainty that the reader-aloud must feel as to where a break or pause is coming, testifies to the genuineness of the poem's impulse. Where its rhythm approaches regularity, as in the second and third stanzas:

> The dew of the morning
>   Sunk chill on my brow—
> It felt like the warning
>   Of what I feel now

the conventionality of the medium becomes more obvious; and we have a sense of the extreme precariousness, the fragility, of this mode of expression, in what is after all a work of immaturity.

A comparison between this poem and *Ae fond kiss* is instructive. (The comparison is suggested, though not elaborated on, by I. A. Richards in *The Principles of Literary Criticism*.) The four famous lines of the latter poem:

> Had we never loved so blindly,
> Had we never been so kindly,
> Never met and never parted,
> We had ne'er been broken-hearted

—these, as Arnold says, are beyond Byron's reach. But after repeated readings of Burns's poem they stand out oddly from the hubbub of stock emotionalism which surrounds them (the 'dark despairs' and all the rest of it.) This contrast, taken with the flaccid, overweight character of the stanza form, suggests an impurity in the poetic impulse; a suggestion which is confirmed (not that confirmation is necessary) by what we know of Burns's attitude in life towards the importunities of 'Nancy'. In Byron's poem, on the other hand, there is no such impurity. It springs from a situation which is felt by the reader as real (whatever the biographical facts may be). And this feeling of reality, together with the immaturity which conditions it, is conveyed in the varying character of the rhythm.

An equal, though different, success is the later lyric *There be none of Beauty's daughters*. Here the constituent of the poem is no more than a gravely conventional compliment, in the Regency manner. The imagery:

> And the midnight moon is weaving
> Her bright chain o'er the deep

is of the same quality as Byron's friend Tom Moore's. The distinctiveness is again in the rhythm and tempo. It is not just in the subtle abrogations of regularity:

> There be none of Beauty's daughters
> ——With a magic like thee;

(Everything is lost, if we make the semantically insignificant change to 'With a magic *like to* thee'.) The charm lies most in the way in which, while the phrasing pays the most graceful homage possible to Miss Clairmont's singing (by announcing that it has made Lord Byron's spirit bow before her, and lulled to rest that oceanic, tempestuous bosom), at the same time those light but subtle changes of tempo acknowledge with an equal grace the essential slightness of the theme. ('A full *but soft* emotion'.) It is in ways like these that Byron's short lyrics at their best may be said to achieve their own kind of decorum, a decorum not deriving from any impersonal convention or established mode. In a piece like *She walks in beauty* we have the nearest that this decorum, while remaining quite personal to Byron, comes to a stylization.

> . . . And all that's best of dark and bright
> Meet in her aspect and her eyes;
> Thus mellow'd to that tender light
> Which heaven to gaudy day denies.
>
> One shade the more, one ray the less,
> Had half impair'd the nameless grace. . . .

This last line quotes Pope, and the manner in general is plainly near to one of Pope's manners:

> So, when the sun's broad beam has tir'd the sight,
> All mild ascends the moon's more sober light;
> Serene in virgin modesty she shines,
> And unobserved the glaring orb declines.

But this air of graceful conformity to a tradition is rare in Byron's lyrics. They are perfectly complete in themselves; but, as a rule, they excite an interest in the poet over and above our admiration of his skill; we feel them to be parts of a whole which is both greater and different. Reading an exquisite poem of Thomas Campion may make us want to read other poems of Campion; but wider reading, while it increases our respect for the poet by revealing the scope of his art, adds nothing to our appreciation of the poem with which we started. And to appreciate that poem rightly is to realize that there is no point in trying to go behind or beyond it. This is not because Campion is 'minor'; we have the same feeling about that great lyric of Dryden *Ah, fading joy*. A lyric of Byron, on the other hand, a lyric like *So we'll go no more a-roving*, the best one he wrote, differs from *Ah, fading joy* or *Rose-cheekt Lawra*, not only in gaining in life and meaning from our sense that it is the culmination of a poet's whole work, but in being on the face of it a dramatic utterance: the voice of an individual.

'Sincerity and strength', was the judgement of Swinburne, endorsed by Arnold; and it brings us again to that personal question, which can never be long postponed, or dodged, in the discussion of Byron. The 'strength', of course, needs little commentary. An athletic buoyancy is the most noticeable, and often the redeeming, feature of Byron's poetry, tempering our exasperation after a long session with the Poetical Works, some of which are bad, and many of which are not very good. He has the extra zest, the record-breaker's enthusiasm, of the lame man exulting in his ability to ride and swim. Sometimes, indeed, this immortal velocity of Byron's causes a comic incongruity between his movement and his matter:

Though wit may flash from fluent lips, and mirth distract the breast,
Through midnight hours that yield no more their former hope of rest;
'Tis but as ivy-leaves around the ruin'd turret wreath,
All green and wildly fresh without, all worn and grey beneath.

And a poem like the one that begins:

Oh, talk to me not of a name great in story;
The days of our youth are the days of our glory;

for all its poignancy as an utterance of the ageing Byron, is, as a piece of verse, an exhilarating gallop. The strength of Byron, then, can show itself in uninteresting or undistinguished ways; but it is an indispensable quality of his best poetry: while it prevents his lesser things from being at any rate tame or dull. Even where the strength is consciously measured and restraining itself, as in the sonnet to George IV ('To be the father of the fatherless'), we see its power when we compare it with Shelley's sonnet *England in 1819*, and this is a poem in which Shelley is uncharacteristically forceful and strong.

'Sincerity', however—that difficult but indispensable concept for the critic—is a more complex matter; all readers of Byron know how awkward is its application to him. For the moment, its reference may be limited to the felt identification of the poet with the emotion expressed. Now it is an interesting, and peculiar, characteristic of some of the greatest things that Byron wrote, that their impressiveness derives partly from our feeling that there is *not* this complete identification. I am thinking particularly of poems associated with the Separation Drama. The explicit emotion—or commotion—is expressed powerfully enough. Byron is much more deeply disturbed than in his earlier poems; there is no question of his acting a part, as in the verse-romances; the expression comes from the centre. And yet we register some consciousness of the writer that there are features of the experience which his present state of mind compels him to leave out, but which will reassert themselves later. Faced with these poems of Byron, poems which have a human and poetic character for which I can think of no parallel, we cannot call them insincere; we are forced, therefore, to revise our notion of sincerity. Consider the *Lines on hearing that Lady Byron was ill*, perhaps the most impressive poem that Byron wrote; since it is not very well known, and I wish to comment on some details, I will quote the whole.

> And thou wert sad—yet I was not with thee;
> And thou wert sick, and yet I was not near;
> Methought that joy and health alone could be
> Where I was *not*—and pain and sorrow here!
> And is it thus?—It is as I foretold,
> And shall be more so; for the mind recoils
> Upon itself, and the wreck'd heart lies cold,
> While heaviness collects the shattered spoils.
> It is not in the storm nor in the strife
> We feel benumb'd, and wish to be no more,
> But in the after-silence on the shore,
> When all is lost, except a little life.
> I am too well avenged!—but 'twas my right;
> Whate'er my sins might be, *thou* wert not sent
> To be the Nemesis who should requite—
> Nor did Heaven choose so near an instrument.
> Mercy is for the merciful!—if thou
> Hast been of such, 'twill be accorded now.
> Thy nights are banish'd from the realms of sleep!—

Yes! they may flatter thee, but thou shalt feel
A hollow agony which will not heal,
For thou art pillow'd on a curse too deep; ·
Thou hast sown in my sorrow, and must reap
The bitter harvest in a woe as real!
I have had many foes, but none like thee;
For 'gainst the rest I could myself defend,
And be avenged, or turn them into friend;
But thou in safe implacability
Hadst nought to dread—in thy own weakness shielded,
And in my love, which hath but too much yielded,
And spared, for thy sake, some I should not spare;
And thus upon the world—trust in thy truth,
And the wild fame of my ungovern'd youth—
On things that were not, and on things that are—
Even upon such a basis hast thou built
A monument, whose cement hath been guilt!
The moral Clytemnestra of thy lord,
And hew'd down, with an unsuspected sword,
Fame, peace, and hope—and all the better life,
Which, but for this cold treason of thy heart,
Might still have risen from out the grave of strife,
And found a nobler duty than to part.
But of thy virtues didst thou make a vice,
Trafficking with them in a purpose cold,
For present anger, and for future gold—
And buying other's grief at any price.
And thus once enter'd into crooked ways,
The earthly truth, which was thy proper praise,
Did not still walk beside thee—but at times,
And with a breast unknowing its own crimes,
Deceit, averments incompatible,
Equivocations, and the thoughts which dwell
In Janus-spirits—the significant eye
Which learns to lie with silence—the pretext
Of prudence, with advantages annex'd—
The acquiescence in all things which tend,
No matter how, to the desired end—
All found a place in thy philosophy.
The means were worthy, and the end is won—
I would not do by thee as thou hast done!

Even without knowledge of the personal situation, the *Sitz im
Leben*, we recognize this as a poem coming straight out of life;
the command of form and expression that makes it a poem being
obviously sustained by an impulse to self-justification *in* life. And

a proper reading could only be done by a reader who grasped that situation. At the same time, different readings—though they would all have to be dramatic ones—could well be effective. Thus, the substance of the poem *appears* to be the expression of a feeling of vindictiveness, together with a demonstrative grounding and rationalization of that feeling. And so it could be plausibly rendered. It develops dramatically, from an anguished effort of self-justification before the 'moral Clytemnestra' to a concentrated and merciless analysis of her character, of which the impulsion is manifestly Byron-Agamemnon's incredulous resentment. It is this impulsion which gives their remarkable force to the closing lines, where the prose-like precision of the writing only heightens our sense of the agonized animosity which pervades the whole:

> Deceit, averments incompatible,
> Equivocations, and the thoughts which dwell
> In Janus-spirits—the significant eye
> Which learns to lie with silence—the pretext
> Of prudence, with advantages annex'd—
> The acquiescence in all things which tend,
> No matter how, to the desired end,—
> All found a place in thy philosophy.

This animosity is the *apparent* substance of the poem. But in its true character, which the proper dramatic reading could bring out, it is surely not so much an expression of hatred, as an expression of the will to feel hatred. That there is, indeed, no conscious criticism of the self-indulgence, is evident in the tense inflexibility of the accent. And it might be protested that, while we know that the vindictiveness is not the whole of the poem, we have to go outside the poem to justify that reading. However, there are signs in the poem itself of good, restorative feelings which are trying, though not successfully, to sustain themselves against the overmastering waves of destructive emotion. Let us imagine that we read the opening, without knowing anything of the situation behind the poem, or guessing what is coming; certainly it is a remonstrance, but could it not sound like a tender one?—

> And thou wert sad—yet I was not with thee;
> And thou wert sick, and yet I was not near;
> Methought that joy and health alone could be
> Where I was *not*—and pain and sorrow here!
> And is it thus?—

With 'It is as I foretold' the vindictiveness asserts itself. Yet the generalized reflection that follows, 'It is not in the storm nor in the strife &c.', again suggests, if not sympathy, at least a recognition of the common humanity of Lady Byron, with a latent sadness that comes to the surface in 'I am too well avenged!' But once again comes the insistence, this time with a significant extra emphasis: 'I am too well avenged!—*but 'twas my right!*' From then on, irritation at the strain of sustaining this implacable attitude of angry righteousness seems to increase the volume and destructiveness of the negative emotions, the indulgence of which is what one's memory chiefly carries away from the poem. And yet, read again with an ear for its true music, does it not convey a Byron who both wants, and does not want, to feel like this? It is a remarkable human document.

As such it prompts us, as Byron's work so insistently does, to biographical conjecture. But it seems to me sufficiently a poem, despite the 'character' terms which analysis of it must require, to be discussed without passing into appraisal of the rights and wrongs of the Separation Drama. So does another poem of this period, the *Epistle to Augusta*, which makes an interesting contrast: here we have a different note:

> The fault was mine; nor do I seek to screen
> My errors with defensive paradox;
> I have been cunning in mine overthrow,
> The careful pilot of my proper woe.
>
> Mine were my faults, and mine be their reward.
> My whole life was a contest, since the day
> That gave me being, gave me that which marr'd
> The gift,—a fate, or will, that walk'd astray. . . .

That 'fate, *or will*', is a relevant comment on the lines on Lady Byron, and 'I have been cunning in mine overthrow', with its suggestion of insight into the nature of masochistic gratification, also suggests something of what has been kept out of the earlier poem, the keeping of it out being possibly the reason for that curious effect of willed inflexibility noted there. True, we can still hear the Byron of *Childe Harold*:

> Kingdoms and empires in my little day
> I have outlived, and yet I am not old;
> And when I look on this, the petty spray
> Of my own years of trouble, which have roll'd
> Like a wild bay of breakers, melts away;
> Something—I know not what—does still uphold
> A spirit of slight patience. . . .

But there is a difference; in spite of 'Something, I know not what . . .', Byron is not offering vagueness as profundity; his uncertainties are frankly uncertainties:

> Surely I once beheld a nobler aim.
> But all is over—I am one the more
> To baffled millions who have gone before.

And correspondingly, his self-knowledge seems deeper and more genuine:

> Had I but sooner learnt the crowd to shun,
> I had been better than I now can be;
> The passions which have torn me would have slept;
> *I* had not suffered, and *thou* hadst not wept.
>
> . . . I have had the share
> Of life which might have fill'd a century,
> Before its fourth in time had pass'd me by.
>
> . . . not in vain,
> Even for its own sake, do we purchase pain.

And comparing the manner with that of the lines on Lady Byron, as well as *Childe Harold*, we notice another difference; the *Epistle* is unmistakably by the same poet, but unlike them it is not declamation; it is, on the whole, restrained and circumstantial. It might be called Byron's *Tintern Abbey*, the nearest he comes to 'emotion recollected in tranquillity'—his affairs usually allowing him little tranquillity to recollect in. And like *Tintern Abbey* it associates the renewal of strength for living with the emotion of love, towards Nature—the 'Nature' of Romantic poets—and towards a sister for whom he has more than the conventional affection of a brother. The comparison with Wordsworth of course reminds us that the two poets are extremely, almost absurdly, unlike: in spite of such lines as these in the *Epistle*:

> Perhaps a kinder clime, or purer air,
> (For even to this may change of soul refer,
> And with light armour we may learn to bear,)
> Have taught me a strange quiet, which was not
> The chief companion of a calmer lot.
>
> I feel almost at times as I have felt
> In happy childhood; trees, and flowers, and brooks,
> Which do remember me of where I dwelt
> Ere my young mind was sacrificed to books,
> Come as of yore upon me. . . .

The world is all before me; I but ask
Of Nature that with which she will comply—

. . . Nor shall I conceal
That with all this I still can look around,
And worship Nature with a thought profound.

But, as the last quotation suggests, Byron's 'Nature' is a shade
perfunctory, and he has not earned, as Wordsworth has, his
right to the word 'profound'. We feel the 'strange quiet' to be
indeed strange, to be but a breathing-space amid storm and
stress. The reassurance and reorientation promised by the Alps
is felt even in the poem as merely temporary; *caelum non animum
mutat* is as true of Byron's wanderings, as of D. H. Lawrence's.

Compared with any passage of *Childe Harold* or the lines on
Lady Byron, the *Epistle* has some variety of tone; but it is still
only the expression of one side of Byron's nature; we feel that
another tone is wanting, and at one moment it seems to be
almost there:

But now I fain would for a time survive,
If but to see what next can well arrive.

Contemplating that rueful humour (*what next?!*) we are reminded at this point that the *Epistle* is written in the stanza of
Don Juan.

But though neither the *Epistle*, nor the *Lines*, are fully representative of Byron's mature genius, they show a great advance
in reality compared with anything he had written earlier; and,
though I have criticized this and that point in their composition,
I should not like to leave them without recording my opinion
that they are the work of a great (if not yet fully developed)
poet. Stylistically, they have one striking feature. The Regency
quality, associated in Byron's verse and prose with an air of
aristocratic recklessness, has disappeared. An urgent personal
pressure has transformed Byron's characteristic way of writing
into a style of no particular 'period' flavour, dateless. It is at
this time that the emancipation effected by 'Wordsworth's trash'
first appears at all decisively in Byron's verse; there is the trace
of a changed sensibility here and there in *The Dream*, which also
belongs to this period (1816):—

And he stood calm and quiet, and he spoke
The fitting vows, but heard not his own words,
And all things reel'd around him; he could see
Not that which was, nor that which should have been—

> But the old mansion, and the accustom'd hall,
> And the remember'd chambers, and the place,
> The day, the hour, the sunshine, and the shade,
> All things pertaining to that place and hour,
> And her who was destiny,—came back
> And thrust themselves between him and the light:
> What business had they there at such a time?

The last line, with its brusque directness of speech, is Byronic, not Wordsworthian; but Wordsworth certainly counts for something in the general manner.

The Regency quality which is so unlike Wordsworth, the aristocratic recklessness of a poem like *English Bards*, returns to Byron's verse in the serio-comic poems which are by common consent his most solid achievement: *Beppo*, the *Vision of Judgment*, and *Don Juan*. But it appears now in a context which, for all its high spirits and geniality, is charged with that fuller sense of the actual world. Mr. Eliot, making the point that a great poet's forms cannot be repeated, remarks that 'you cannot write satire in the line of Pope or the stanza of Byron'. 'Satire' seems as good a word as any to describe these extravaganzas, but 'the stanza of Byron' needs further commentary; everything that needs to be said about Byron's later poetry can be said in terms of what he does with that 'stanza'. The great technical freedom of his comic poems corresponds to the spirit in which they were written, one which allowed for great variety of moods, whose swift changes and oscillations now for the first time find expression in Byron's verse.

It is usual to account for the manner of *Beppo* and *Don Juan* by referring to Byron's attachment to Italy; first as the English milord enjoying—perhaps not so much as he sometimes claims —his Venetian emancipation from English stuffiness; and then as the *inglese italianato* in the milieu of Teresa Guiccioli, a participator not only in the patriotic conspiracies of Italy, but in Italian domesticity. (See *The Last Attachment*, by Iris Origo.) And these new associations, together with his interest in the comic poetry of the Italian Renaissance, certainly colour the lively and picturesque surface of those poems. But the core of *Don Juan* is still Byron's preoccupation with England, and with himself as he was, and might have been, and might still be, in England. And with this particular preoccupation there goes a general concern for truth and reality, expressed either as an impatient moral and social criticism, or as a literary protest: he uses poetry for the expression of anti-poetic sentiments. What is often in itself gay story-telling, or down-to-earth humour, or sentimental inconsequence, or Romantic bravura, or brusque sarcasm, or just pure fun and high spirits, is underlined and given point by this constant appeal to a standard of truth in life and literature. There is an incidental comparison and contrast here between Byron's development and that of Shelley and Keats. In their later work, in *The Triumph of Life* and the revised *Hyperion*, there are signs, interesting to the few who are interested in literary criticism, that the acceptance of a stricter criterion of reality is associated with a need for greater technical control in the versification. They turn, not to the comic Italian poets, but to Petrarch and Dante. Now in Byron—though he too wrote his *Prophecy of Dante*, in *terza rima*—a contrasting process occurs. The new development is not so much a technical development, as a disdain of technique in the ordinary sense. But the purpose likewise is to secure the maximum directness and realism of presentation.

However, it must be granted that the reality in which Byron was interested was sometimes of a more mundane order than that which concerned Keats and Shelley. Byron can be preoccupied with the actual at quite a humdrum level. For instance, he has a love of literalness, and a passion for facts; he rebukes Bacon and Voltaire for their historical inaccuracies, which he demonstrates in detail; and he is imaginatively moved when in Venice, not at all by the thought of Shylock or Othello, who are fiction, but only by the history of the Republic. The literal-mindedness can show itself in odd ways, and at surprising moments. 'They mean to *insurrect* here, and are to honour me with a call thereupon,' he broods in his Journal of 9 January 1821. 'I shall not fall back; though I don't think them in force or heart sufficient to make much of it.' Now, as often in Byron, the misgivings of practicality are overcome by a calling up of emotional reserves.

But, *onward!*—it is now the time to act, and what signifies *self*, if a single spark of that which would be worthy of the past can be bequeathed unquenchedly to the future? It is not one man, nor a million, but the *spirit* of liberty which must be spread. The waves which dash upon the shore are, one by one, broken, but yet the *ocean* conquers, nevertheless. It overwhelms the Armada, it wears the rock, and, if the *Neptunians* are to be believed, it has not only destroyed, but made a world. In like manner, whatever the sacrifice of individuals, the great cause will gather strength, sweep down what is rugged, and fertilize (for *sea-weed* is *manure*) what is cultivable.

This impassioned meditation, on a cosmic theme, into which the personal preoccupation develops, comes from the grand, the European Byron, the great human force in the world, who is well qualified to command that admiration and loyalty of which Santayana speaks. But the point I want to make is that that last touch ('for *sea-weed* is *manure*'), in such a context, is equally characteristic, and equally admirable. It is a quality without which we would not have had *Don Juan*.

But of course the truthfulness of *Don Juan* is not so much this literalism, and still less the intenser, higher-order truth to life which preoccupied Keats and Shelley; it is man-of-the-world realism; and as such Byron defends the poem, with suitable frankness, in a letter to Kinnaird. 'As to "Don Juan", confess, confess—you dog and be candid—that it is the sublime of *that there* sort of writing—it may be bawdy but is it not good English? It may be profligate but is it not *life*, is it not the thing? Could any man have written it who has not lived in the world? —and fooled in a post-chaise?—in a hackney coach?—in a gondola?—against a wall?—in a court carriage?—in a vis à vis?—on a table?—and under it?' Yet even here, in that proximity of 'life', 'the thing', 'lived in the world', to 'good English', there is a literary manifesto. And in the general attitude there is a moral intention, which Arnold perceived in Byron, though he did not explicitly refer to *Don Juan*. 'The truth is', Byron wrote to Murray during the Pope controversy, 'that in these days the grand *primum mobile* of England is *cant*; cant political, cant religious, cant moral; but always *cant*, multiplied through all the varieties of life. It is the fashion. . .' That the fashion does not change so very much, is one reason why *Don Juan* is still lively reading. There are still enough shabby smugnesses at home, and tyrannies abroad, to preserve its astringency and ensure its tonic effect. In this moral attitude, and in the tone of voice in which it is conveyed, Byron reminds us of Burns, with whom indeed he felt an affinity. 'Burns,' he says, comparing him to the Cockney School, 'is often coarse, but never vulgar.' And again: 'Read Burns to-day. What would he have been, if a patrician? We should have had more polish—less force—just as much verse, but no immortality—a divorce and a duel or two, the which had he survived, as his potations must have been less spirituous, he might have lived as long as Sheridan.'[1] But this last comment also registers Byron's sense of his difference from Burns. For all they have in common, in their man-to-man appeal, their amatory inflammability, their satiric bent, and their

[1] Journal, 16 Nov. 1813.

invocation of the universal human heart—and also, it may be, a national characteristic which comes out in all these traits— Byron remains the 'patrician', speaking from the plane of Sheridan, not that of Burns; there is something dignified about his dissipation, even while there is something of *l'homme sensuel moyen* about his dignity.

It is not, then, from his admiration for Burns, nor even from his interest in the Italian poets, that Byron's comic poetry derives its inspiration and sanction; but from the use of resources in Byron himself, which he had not previously exploited in poetry. The Byron of the letters and journals, of the world in which he was worried and was bored, and sneered and gossiped, comes into the verse; to provide the standards by which Wordsworth or Wilberforce, George IV or the Duke of Wellington, are judged. In the *Vision of Judgment* it is the demeanour of Wilkes, besides that of Junius ('I loved my country, and I hated him'), that attracts Byron; while in *Beppo* the viewpoint is that of the amused and amusing cosmopolitan Englishman, observing Venetian sexual *mores*, with their matter-of-factness and good sense. The extension of range appears poetically as that ability to modulate, or to pass from key to key without modulation, which constantly appears in the letters; here, for example, is the conclusion of a letter to Moore (Venice, 19 Sept. 1818.)

I wish you good-night, with a Venetian benediction, *Benedetto te, e la terra che farà!* 'May you be blessed, and the earth which you will *make!*'— is it not pretty? You would think it prettier still, if you had heard it, as I did two hours ago, from the lips of a Venetian girl, with large black eyes, a face like Faustina's, and the figure of a Juno—tall and energetic as a Pythoness, with eyes flashing, and her dark hair streaming in the moonlight—one of those women who may be made anything. I am sure that if I put a poniard into the hand of this one, she would plunge it where I told her—and into *me*, if I offended her. I like this kind of animal, and am sure that I should have preferred Medea to any woman that ever breathed. You may, perhaps, wonder that I don't in that case . . . I could have forgiven the dagger and the bowl,—any thing, but the deliberate desolation piled upon me, when I stood alone upon my hearth, with my household gods shivered around me. Do you suppose I have forgotten it? It has comparatively swallowed up in me every other feeling, and I am only a spectator upon earth, till a tenfold opportunity offers. It may come yet. There are more to be blamed than   , and it is on these that my eyes are fixed unceasingly.

Here the accent of the final sentences strikes us, not as a sudden reversal of feeling, but as the disentangling of a feeling that is already a constituent of the half-humorous, half-Romantic description of the Venetian girl. A finer example is what follows an impassioned defence of Sheridan's character, as a type of the gentleman-adventurer of genius; when there emerges, in a beautiful way, the general sense of life, at once melancholy and admiring, which gives depth to it.

Were his [Sheridan's] intrigues more notorious than those of all his contemporaries? and is his memory to be blasted, and theirs respected? Don't let yourself be led away by clamour, but compare him with the coalitioner Fox, and the pensioner Burke, as man of principle, and with none in talent, for he beat them all *out* and *out*. Without means, without connexion, without character (which might be false at first, and make him mad afterwards in desperation), he beat them all, in all he ever attempted. But alas, poor human nature! Good-night, or rather, morning. It is four, and the dawn gleams over the Grand Canal, and unshadows the Rialto. I must to bed; up all night—but, as George Philpot says, 'it's life, though, damme it's life!'

It is a way of life that Byron is defending here, and the reference to it is one of the positive criteria of judgement in *Don Juan*. The other, of course, is Byron's Romanticism; the Romantic self which Byron had not so much outgrown, as come to see for one acting-part among others. And the success of *Don Juan* is mainly a matter of Byron's success in effecting a positive relation between the two. The poem is a triumph of personality.

The relation between the Romantic-tragic and the sophisticated-cynical appears in a simple form in the story of Juan's father. This is the conclusion:

> It was a trying moment that which found him
> Standing alone beside his desolate hearth,
> Where all his household gods lay shiver'd round him;
> No choice was left his feelings or his pride,
> But death or Doctors' Commons—so he died.

The predominant effect is of the Byronic obsession; Byron is still mowing the aftermath of the Separation Drama. But the effect is of course qualified by the manner of its introduction ('It was a trying moment . . .'), which invites the attitude of ironic detachment; and the astringent terseness of the last couplet is reminiscent of George Crabbe, whose poetry Byron admired. This manner of dealing with his troubles is obvious; but often, especially in the digressive passages, the effect is more complex. Consider the celebrated outburst towards the end of Canto I. Here Byron has been alluding to the adverse reception he expects to get, as a 'dissenting author', from the *Edinburgh* and *Quarterly*, and quoting Horace (*Non ego hoc ferrem calida juventa Consule Planco*) adds that in his 'hot youth' he 'would not have brooked at all this sort of thing', 'being most ready to return a blow'. Now we see Byron's way of picking up a theme for extensive development; the interest of such passages is partly that we do not know *which* element will be picked up. 'Hot youth', in its Horatian context, here becomes the theme, and is developed, at first with a little irony:

> But now at thirty years my hair is gray—
> (I wonder what it will be like at forty?
> I thought of a peruke the other day),
> My heart is not much greener; and in short, I
> Have squander'd my whole summer while 'twas May,
> And feel no more the spirit to retort; I
> Have spent my life, both interest and principal,
> And deem not, what I deem'd, my soul invincible.

We notice the off-hand rhymes, 'forty', 'short, I', 'retort; I'. Then the irony vanishes, in a full-volumed Romanticism; as usual in *Don Juan*, the modulation is signalized by a change in the character of the rhymes, and the general sonority: the voice, though remaining a speaking voice, takes on an underlying singing-tone:

> No more—no more—Oh! never more on me
> The freshness of the heart can fall like dew,
> Which out of all the lovely things we see
> Extracts emotions beautiful and new;
> Hived in our bosoms like the bag o' the bee.
> Think'st thou the honey with those objects grew?
> Alas! 'twas not in them, but in thy power
> To double even the sweetness of a flower.

It is Byron's equivalent to *Dejection: an Ode*. But the stanza just quoted is followed by a partial return of the common-sense, the reasonable, the Augustan, emerging ruefully in a still predominantly Romantic context:

> No more—no more—Oh! never more, my heart,
> Canst thou be my sole world, my universe!
> Once all in all, but now a thing apart,
> Thou canst not be my blessing or my curse:
> The illusion's gone for ever, and thou art
> Insensible, I trust, but none the worse,
> And in thy stead I've got a deal of judgment,
> Though heaven knows how it ever found a lodgment.

'*None the worse*': the very un-sonorous rhyme of 'judgment/ lodgment' gives the manner. This returning reasonableness takes on a colour of light irony:

> My days of love are over; me no more
> The charms of maid, wife, and still less of widow
> Can make the fool of which they did before—
> In short, I must not lead the life I did do;
> The credulous hope of mutual minds is o'er,
> The copious use of claret is forbid too;
> So, for a good old-gentlemanly vice,
> I think I must take up with avarice.

The Horatian regret (*nec spes animi mutua creduli*) appears as a foil to middle-aged matter-of-factness; the stanza running out into flippancy.

The return to the general manner of the poem is effected in an interesting way. There is first a surprise turn: a blast on the trombone of *Childe Harold*:

> Ambition was my idol, which was broken
> Before the shrines of Sorrow, and of Pleasure;

But this leads into four lines, neither ironic nor Romantic, though serious enough:

> And the two last have left me many a token
> O'er which reflection may be made at leisure;
> Now, like Friar Bacon's brazen head, I've spoken,
> 'Time is, Time was, Time's past':

and these serve as a bridge passage to the conclusion, or culmination:

> . . . a chymic treasure
> Is glittering youth, which I have spent betimes—
> My heart in passion, and my head on rhymes.

This culmination is Romantic in feeling; but the Romanticism is subtly qualified by the reversion to a completely Augustan manner, a Popean neatness:

> . . . glittering youth, which I have spent betimes—
> My heart in passion, and my head on rhymes.

The general nature of the effect is obvious without all this analysis, but analysis perhaps serves to bring out the peculiar significance, the dramatic force, of that closing couplet. The Romantic and the Augustan come together with an air of momentary reconciliation; nostalgia for lost youth, for the loss

of the emotional spontaneity and power of empathy that belong
to youth, is accommodated to a practical acceptance of reality;
giving the effect of a resolution (*Aufhebung*) of the two contrasting
attitudes on which the passage is built. This dialectic is the life
of *Don Juan*.

It may be worth adding that neither the Romanticism, nor
the irony, nor their coming from the same poet, is specifically
Byronic. There is such a thing as Romantic irony, as in Heine
or Musset. What *is* highly personal to Byron, is the temporary
stabilization of conflicting emotions, in a manner which is
neither Romantic nor ironical. There is no calculation, of course,
in this effect, but in all the wayward progress of the verse there
is an internal control which is lacking in other semi-serious
poetry, W. H. Auden's for example; the poet knows what he is
doing; at any given moment he knows just how serious, or how
un-serious, he is.

In range and variety of emotional tone, as in other respects,
Don Juan is the antithesis of *The Prelude*. One difficulty in reading
the latter is Wordsworth's habit of moving placidly on from dull
passages, or passages of fair to middling interest, to inspired passages, without break, transposition, or change of gear. In *Don
Juan* Byron has solved for himself and his purposes, as Wordsworth in my opinion did not, the problem of the long poem.
His solution is to come forward frankly as an improviser.

> I don't know that there may be much ability
> Shown in this sort of desultory rhyme;
> But there's a conversational facility,
> Which may round off an hour upon a time.
> Of this I'm sure at least, there's no servility
> In mine irregularity of chime,
> Which rings what's uppermost of new or hoary,
> Just as I feel the *Improvvisatore*.

One need not dwell on the dangers and temptations of the
Improvvisatore in poetry. Perhaps his most tiresome characteristic
is Byron's recurrent self-satisfaction that, without taking any
pains, he is writing better poetry than his fellow poets who
do. This makes him the victim of a technique, or lack of technique, which permits him not only to tolerate second-rateness
but elaborate it with gusto.

> Who holds the balance of the world? Who reign
> O'er congress, whether royalist or liberal?
> Who rouse the shirtless patriots of Spain?

(That make old Europe's journals squeak and gibber all),
Who keep the world, both old and new, in pain
Or pleasure? Who makes politics run glibber all?
The shade of Buonaparte's noble daring?
Jew Rothschild, and his fellow-Christian, Baring.

The nullity of the writing appropriately accompanies the sentiment of a writer in *Gringoire*. At the other extreme, there are
many lapses into the histrionic-profound, from which Byron is
never free in any of his work, 'Between two worlds life hovers
like a star' and all the rest of it; unimaginable from a poet like
Leopardi, beside whom, with all his bookishness, Byron often
seems an essentially uneducated spirit.

But the aplomb of the improviser, and the reader's awareness
of it, are essential to the art of a poem which Hazlitt described,
felicitously, as 'a poem about itself'.

> But Adeline was not indifferent: for
> (*Now* for a commonplace!) beneath the snow,
> As a volcano holds the lava more
> Within—*et caetera*. Shall I go on? No,
> I hate to hunt down a tired metaphor,
> So let the often-used volcano go,
> Poor thing! How frequently, by me and others,
> It hath been stirred up till its smoke quite smothers!
>
> I'll have another figure in a trice—
> What say you to a bottle of champagne?
> Frozen into a very vinous ice,
> Which leaves few drops of that immortal rain,
> Yet in the very centre, past all price,
> About a liquid glassful will remain;
> And this is stronger than the strongest grape
> Could e'er express in its expanded shape.

Byron's improvisation here, after the hit at conventional poetry,
his own included, is a justification in practice of figures drawn
from 'Art', rather than 'Nature', Pope's use of which he defended
against Bowles. But the important point about it is this: the
false start shows not only the slip into commonplace which he
notices, but an inability which he was perhaps not conscious of,
to concentrate his effects; he needs space to be a poet. This of
course has bearings on the lack of a distinctive diction, noted
earlier. A poet like Keats might have done something with that
'volcano'; Byron could not, but he turns his incapacity into a
virtue by rejecting the figure in full view of the reader.

And in fact Byron is perpetually aware, unlike Wordsworth, or the Tennyson of *In Memoriam*, that he has a reader. Then, his sociable tone, his friendship with that reader, is founded on the tacit agreement that he too is a fellow sinner.

> They [the sailors] vow to amend their lives, and yet they don't;
> Because if drown'd they can't; if spared, they won't.

And Malthus does the thing 'gainst which he writes.

We know what human nature is like, and have not too exalted a conception of it; since we ourselves are the examples that we know most intimately. The air of nonchalant familiarity, which finds its sanction in this fellow-feeling, is not un-Augustan; but it is nearer to Dryden than to Pope. And this is not the only way in which the Regency, as illustrated by Byron, reminds us of the Restoration. But Byron's true analogue in Restoration poetry is not Dryden but Rochester.

> Without, or with, offence to friends and foes,
> I sketch your world exactly as it goes.

'Without, *or with*' is the touch of recklessness typical of Byron; but it reminds us also of the isolated, anarchic flouting of society which we often find in Rochester, and never in Dryden. There are interesting social and political parallels, as well as personal and poetic ones, between these two rebellious patricians of different epochs; quite apart from their aristocratic anarchism and will to *épater le bourgeois*, there are likenesses between the Rochester seen by Bishop Burnet, and the Byron seen by Dr. Kennedy.

But this debonair freedom, and the ease with which Byron manages his transitions and expatiates at whatever length he pleases, and on whatever occasion, about anything which interests him—none of these vivacities convince us that the poet is always enjoying himself. He is not always letting himself go with such satisfaction as he shows in the flyting of Southey. His success in elevating drunken inconsequence to the status of art, is itself as much a product of the unhappy libertine's trying to persuade himself that he is cheerful, as of the half-earnest moralist's ambition to be serious. Even his fun is more the evidence of a gay, than of a cheerful, temperament. It is not hard to see a desperately uncomfortable man in the author of *Don Juan*; the very writing of it is part of the attempt to cheer himself up.

> And if I laugh at any mortal thing,
> 'Tis that I may not weep.

The switches and reversals of mood are not so much the result of a critical check upon his emotion, as a flinching away from it; he hastens to a superficial kind of self-revelation, for fear of a deeper self-betrayal. Sometimes he seems actually frightened by a thought that has arisen in composition. The strange opening of Canto XIV, with the typical change between stanzas vi and vii, is a case in point; and earlier in the poem, after a moving rendering of the madness and death of Haidée, he intervenes with:

> But let me change this theme, which grows too sad,
> And lay this sheet of sorrows on the shelf;
> I don't much like describing people mad,
> For fear of seeming rather touch'd myself—

And a similar fear seems to spring up, when he has let himself go in some tender sentiment, of a kind which he will commit to verse, though rarely to prose; but will be quick to abandon, if he thinks he is being caught out, or 'placed' in any single attitude. Indeed, one of his unpleasant traits of character, the caddishness that he showed in the Guiccioli episode (in his letters to friends), seems to be due, not merely to an obvious dislike of ridicule, but to this fear of being 'typed', thought of as committed to any one part—especially if it is undignified: among the Christian virtues which Mr. Wilson Knight has found in Byron, indifference about one's personal dignity was not included.

But the great self-release Byron gets in *Don Juan* is only possible when he gives up his dignity as a poet. This is interestingly shown in the *ubi sunt* passage in Canto XI. Juan's presence in England leads Byron to moralize, in a gruesome-cum-humorous manner, on 'the life of a young noble'. After an epigrammatic stanza describing this (lxxv) the thought of the personal application of these lines provokes him to an exercise in the histrionic-profound:

> 'Where is the world?' cries Young, at *eighty*—'Where
> The world in which a man was born?' Alas!
> Where is the world of *eight* years past? '*Twas there*—
> I look for it—'tis gone, a globe of glass!
> Crack'd, shiver'd, vanish'd, scarcely gazed on, ere
> A silent change dissolves the glittering mass.

These lines, and there are many like them in *Don Juan*, incite us to a use of Goethe's comment: 'When he reflects, he is a child.' The inability to think is as evident as the jerky, straining motion, and, as the italics betray, Byron is trying to compensate by an

imposed emphasis and gesture for his failure to realize his elusive
subject. Against his excited gesticulating we may place two lines
from a Shakespeare sonnet:

> Ah, yet doth beauty, like a dial-hand,
> Steal from his figure, and no pace perceived.

In Byron's lines, it is the generality of the concept of Time that
defeats him; his poetic gift only appears when he gets down to
particulars.

> Where is Napoleon the Grand? God knows;
> Where little Castlereagh? The devil can tell:
> Where Grattan, Curran, Sheridan, all those
> Who bound the bar or senate in their spell?
> Where is the unhappy Queen, with all her woes?
> And where the Daughter, whom the Isles loved well?
> Where are those martyr'd saints the Five per Cents?
> And where—oh, where the devil are the Rents?
>
> Where's Brummel? Dish'd. Where's Long Pole Wellesley? Diddled.
> Where's Whitbread? Romilly? Where's George the Third?
> Where is his will? (That's not so soon unriddled.)
> And where is 'Fum' the Fourth, our 'royal bird'?
> Gone down, it seems, to Scotland to be fiddled
> Unto by Sawney's violin, we have heard:
> 'Caw me, caw thee'—for six months hath been hatching
> This scene of royal itch and loyal scratching.
>
> Where is Lord This? And where my Lady That?
> The Honourable Mistresses and Misses?
> Some laid aside like an old Opera hat,
> Married, unmarried, and remarried (this is
> An evolution oft performed of late),
> Where are the Dublin shouts—and London hisses?
> Where are the Grenvilles? Turn'd as usual. Where
> My friends the Whigs? Exactly where they were.

The spacious movement ('. . . queens, patriots, kings, And
dandies, all are gone on the wind's wings') is broken up into
staccato, as with a crash of cymbals. His pen then runs away
with him; the freedom of the *ottava rima* is exploited to the full;
the incoherence of the stanza on Time returns, but this time
incoherence has a dramatic effect—the random snatching at
names evocative of grandeur and gossip, heroes and faded
dandies, scandal and tragedy, triviality and History, which gives
such a hop-skip-and-jump to the movement, only enhances the

amusing reversal at the close: the exemption of the Whigs, with
their permanence of *vis inertiae*, only adds extra sparkle to the
whirligig. Byron has here made a virtue out of his inability to
concentrate his thoughts, to realize the idea of Time either in a
telling image, or a pregnant abstraction; we are to feel his
resilience to the solemn commonplace, in his capacity to organize
a movement of so prodigiously long a wave-length; we ride the
thought on a roller-coaster, not knowing when the next lift or
bump is coming, and emerge exhilarated at the place from which
we started.

The whole performance is admirably dramatic. And here we
have a word that must, after all, be used of Byron. An agreement
between Mr. Wilson Knight and Byron's more conventional
biographers, is their common recognition of this quality in his
behaviour and life-style. 'And each man in his life plays many
parts.' On that question of Byron's sincerity, touched on earlier,
the comparison with a dramatic performer throws some light.
It is possible, in watching a great actor, to respond simul-
taneously in two ways: 'How moving!' and 'How well he plays
his part!' And we should not feel the actor's greatness less, were
we to infer a corresponding duality of consciousness in him.
There is no question of insincerity; the performance is successful
or unsuccessful, good or bad, but it is not sincere or insincere.
Success is a matter of being able to mobilize emotions which
one has either had, or can imagine having, without necessarily
having them at the moment. This is in a sense a commonplace
about Byron. But not all his critics have recognized, as Mr.
Wilson Knight clearly has, that there are distinctions to be made
here between great acting, attitudinizing, and 'putting on an
act'. To judge Byron fairly we have to set aside what is mere
theatricality, or neurosis, the reduplication of an already existent
pattern, and recognize what is in effect a *new* emotion, in
responding to which we are appreciating a conscious art. Some
of Byron's worst attitudinizing occurs when he is least conscious
of it; greater consciousness means greater sincerity, but not in
the sense of a fuller identification of the poet with the explicit
state of feeling; it shows itself rather in an unusual *directness*,
which gives an exceptional artistic distinction to the familiar show
of strength. (I am thinking here of passages like Canto XIV,
stanzas i to xii.)

It is relevant here to mention Byron's interest in the theatre
(he was on the management committee of Drury Lane for a
time) and to say a word about his plays. When we look at these,

a likely expectation is not fulfilled. We shall be surprised, if we turn to *Marino Faliero* or *Sardanapalus* in the desire, or dread, of an emotional debauch. The objection to these plays is quite otherwise; they are too analytic, too schematized; we are offered the analysis of dramatic characters and situations, whose presence is a mere intellectual postulate. The plays none the less have some interest, as a serious and conscious attempt at classical strictness in English drama; they consist in a dramatic rhetoric of ideas (or ideologies) belonging to the nineteenth century, but presented in conformity with canons of taste that Corneille might have approved. The intention is worth study: but few will agree with Mr. Wilson Knight that the achievement is that of a great dramatist. The ideas, the situations, and the characters are of a piece with the quality of the verse, and the verse is the verse of Byron. True, there is no necessary connexion between dramatic effectiveness and the Elizabethan stage tradition which Byron refused to revive in his own plays. Nor is there an *a priori* objection to the lucid explicitness of his language, and the severe formality of his dramatic structure. The objection refers to their compatibility with Byron's genius as a whole. In order to subdue his matter to his purpose, and find matter which would suit such a purpose, Byron has to leave out nearly everything that makes him interesting. His genius needed, besides a frame of strictness, rationality, and restraint to enclose it, a world of landscape, disorder, and 'hamming' in which to let itself go. We can go from some letters of Byron to the prose speeches of Hamlet without a jar or sense of transition; we may feel that Byron could have been a character in Shakespeare's plays; but he could not have been a character in one of Byron's. The dramatic gift of Byron is not in his plays, but in his letters and journals; and in the dramatic monody of *Don Juan*.

About the narrative and action of *Don Juan*, it is not necessary to go into detail; their attractions are obvious; and the most original feature of Byron's enterprise is well suggested in this quotation from Halévy's Preface to his *History of the English People in 1815*:

To an Englishman, English society is the whole of society, the ideal society. Buckle, in a work celebrated half a century ago, avowedly treated all forms of human civilisation as so many deviations from the true norm of civilisation, the civilisation of Great Britain. Very different is the attitude of the observer from abroad. A great number of characteristics which, being familiar to the natives from birth, have come to form part of their intellectual and moral nature, are for him matter of

astonishment—whether of admiration or disapproval is indifferent—
and demand from him an explanation. Indeed, of all the nations in
Europe, it is perhaps the English whose institutions must, in many
respects, be regarded as being, beyond the institutions of other people,
paradoxical, 'unique'.

The later cantos of *Don Juan*, and especially the description of
the house-party, owe their excellence to Byron's ability to be
both inside and outside the people, the institutions, and the
social falsities and absurdities, which supply his material. At
home in no civilization himself, he responds the more keenly to
the comic aspect of people who are at home in theirs. In serious
moods, he reveals himself as a *déraciné* who cannot forget 'Society'
and his triumphs and disasters in it, but who dreams of another
kind of society in which the standards of success or failure are
different. That there is an element of day-dream in his fondness
for the viewpoint of a Tartar chieftain, or a levelling radical,
does not mean that he cannot thereby project a lively criticism
of the unrealities, fallacies, and inhumanities of the established
fact: his knowledge of 'life' and 'the world' protects him from
many illusions; and his indulgences in misanthropy do not preclude a real and generous humanity. The anger and horror of
the war sections of *Don Juan* owe the power of their expression
to their being the correlates of positive attitudes; just as the
force of the irony, in the frivolous parts of the poem, derives
from Byron's unfailing capacity to discriminate between the
'human' values and the 'social' ones. And thus it is that *Don
Juan*, which in one aspect is licentious, cynical, antinomian, in
another aspect is a most edifying and improving work.

As to the nominal hero of the poem, objections have been
made to his general colourlessness, passivity, and silence; but he
plays the part that is allotted to him. He seems in his love-affairs
to represent that willingness of Byron to be *used* by women,
which is so curious a quality of Byron's own *vie amoureuse*; but he
never evinces the reaction against that role, and against the
Regency gentleman-amorist in general, which is equally characteristic and significant. So his performance, as a dramatization
of Byron's own relations with women, is always simplified and
partial. Thus, if we judge that his relationship to Catherine II
reflects—as it probably does—Byron's affair with Lady Oxford,
we must add at once that the fiction leaves out something
essential to the understanding of the life-situation: Byron's need
for, or intermittent conviction of his need for, a woman who
would be motherly without moralizing. There are two reasons,

one technical, and one biographical, for this two-dimensional character of the hero. In so far as the traditional Don Juan is part of the conception, Byron the narrator has taken over his functions; and in so far as he stands for the young Byron, the older man is too remote from him (except in the early cantos) to be willing, or perhaps able, to recapture either his foolishness or his charm. The Byron of *Don Juan* does not give us, as does Stendhal, that re-creation of the follies of youth which is done from within, but which we none the less feel to be always under the eyes of maturity. For Byron, the contemplation of the past is too painful; he has too much a sense of loss, and of tragic waste, to accept it as a condition of the present. *Don Juan* is the work of a mature mind, but not one with an integral vision.

And this is, finally, why we cannot rank it very high among the great creative works of literature. 'He did not respect himself, or his art, as much as they deserved'; great art cannot be made out of a boredom with oneself, which is expressed as a boredom with one's subject-matter; and the later cantos of *Don Juan*, which are the finest and most mature parts of the poem, are also, significantly, the parts in which that distaste, that boredom, is becoming a settled attitude.

> But 'why then publish?'—There are no rewards,
> Of fame or profit when the world grows weary.
> I ask in turn,—Why do you play at cards?
> Why drink? Why read?—To make some hour less dreary.
> It occupies me to turn back regards
> On what I've seen or ponder'd, sad or cheery;
> And what I write I cast upon the stream,
> To swim or sink—I have had at least my dream. (XIV. xi)

Byron may get relief from his boredom by writing about it; but this state of mind is incompatible with a sustained creative art. His desire and will to ground Romanticism on reality cannot be satisfied with the attempt to do this in art; he feels that it must be done in life, and it must be done in spite of that nagging fear (exceptionally poignant in one who makes a cult of the spontaneous) of emotional inadequacy. This comes out, not only in the grumbling passages of *Don Juan*, but, with a very pathetic accent, in the very late poem, *On this day I complete my thirty-sixth year*; which was written in Greece.

That reminder of Byron's last service, in the flesh, to the cause of national freedom, induces the suitably sympathetic spirit in which to ask: what is the value of Byron's poetry? what does he leave us with? It is not a question of ranking him among poets;

as Byron himself says in his 1813 Journal, 'Surely the field of
thought is infinite; what does it signify who is before or behind,
in a race which has no goal?' But whether we are to revere him
as an oracle, or regard him, dispassionately or sympathetically,
as a human case, is not a question that can be lightly dismissed.
Byron's personal predicament is certainly there:

> . . . I am one the more
> To baffled millions who have gone before.

And it certainly accounts for many of the weaknesses of his work;
the egocentricity, the grandiloquence, the failures in self-knowledge, the lack of balance and perspective, the ensuing monotony.
But I have tried to show that even in his morose or destructive
moods, even in works that reveal his spiritual malaise most
clearly, there is an opposite movement towards restorativeness
and health. He is a poet not only in that (to use a convenient
vulgarism) he 'gets across' his egoistic passions; he conveys along
with them, though doubtless unwittingly, a sense that his
vehement indulgence in them is, deep down, against the grain.
And our recognition of this ultimate probity is allied to our
pleasure in Byron's vitality. Whether one should go farther than
that, and find in Byron the poet a moral hero, a religious and
spiritual force, I am doubtful; is he coherent enough to command that kind or degree of reverence? I should prefer to say
that at his best he leaves us with a heightened realization of the
value of *personality*, in the sense in which this is distinguished from
character. But of course the two are not to be finally separated.
And to admit this is also a tribute to Byron. His human and
poetic sins are many; but, as with some characters in the *Inferno*,
we dare not view them with patronage, any more than we wish
to mitigate them with pity. It is Byron's attainment of the tragic
that enables him to wring this paradoxical victory out of defeat.

> Poi si rivolse, e parve di coloro
> che corrono a Verona il drappo verde
> per la campagna; e parve di costoro
> Quegli che vince e non colui che perde.